HERE FOR YOU

*How the Art of Being Present
Plays a Role in Healing*

HERE FOR YOU

HOW THE ART OF BEING PRESENT PLAYS A ROLE IN HEALING

MICHELLE M. HARRIS

Here For You: How The Art of Being Present Plays a Role in Healing

Copyright © 2020 by Michelle Harris All rights reserved

No part of this book may be used or reproduced in any manner whatsoever without written permission except in the case of brief quotations embodied in critical articles and reviews.

FIRST EDITION

Book design by M. Rofie Adnan

Edited by Nikki Wright

ISBN 978-1-736-32360-1

Scriptures are from the King James Bible unless otherwise indicated.

Scripture taken from the New King James Version®. Copyright © 1982 by Thomas Nelson. Used by permission. All rights reserved.

Scripture taken from the Holy Bible, New International Version®, NIV®. Copyright © 1973, 1978, 1984, 2011 by Biblica, Inc.™ Used by permission of Zondervan. All rights reserved worldwide. www.zondervan.com The "NIV" and "New International Version" are trademarks registered in the United States Patent and Trademark Office by Biblica, Inc.™

Scripture taken from the Amplified Bible, Copyright © 1954, 1958, 1962, 1964, 1965, 1987 by The Lockman Foundation. Used by permission.

*To my supportive and encouraging husband
Paul Harris and my 3 favorite boys in the world;
Gabriel, Matthias and Ezran.*

Contents

Foreword xiii
Acknowledgments xv
Introduction xix

Part I
Grief
    1: The Reality of Grief 3
    2: The Idea of Moving On. 9

Part II
The Art of Being Present
    3: Identifying Your Motivation 17
    4: Being Present. 19
    5: Exercising Patience 21
    6: Extending Empathy 25
    7: Practical Ways to Help 27

Part III
Considerations
    8: Identifying When we Can't Help 33
    9: When They Don't Want to Talk. 35
    10: Avoiding Trigger Words 37
    11: Speaking Life into Grief 39

Conclusion 41
Reference 43
Memorial 45

Foreword

The inescapable and insufferable pain of loss touches all of our lives. To witness the trauma and brokenness pain confers upon the human heart and emotion can make anyone feel helpless or at a loss for words. However, the impact of expressed care or support are some of the most unselfish and authentic ways to extend the best of ourselves to those living their toughest moments.

Here for You serves as an open call to empathy for those willing to answer. We have a responsibility to care for one another and the information Michelle Harris offers is eye opening and personal. Her openness about her own experiences gives insight into grief while sharing practical approaches to support. Sometimes the greatest care is so simple it can be overlooked. Michelle shines a light on those areas so nothing is missed.

I've known Michelle for over 15 years and she is the real deal. I and so many others have been on the receiving end of her genuine acts of kindness first hand. When I gave birth to my son prematurely and had to walk out of the hospital empty handed, it was a pain like no other. I was overwhelmed and inconsolable. The last thing I wanted while grieving was to be bombarded with inconsiderate questions, put on a strong face for the well-meaning, or feel I was alone in my suffering. Her acts of compassion towards me, even from a distance, so I could heal at my own pace and in my own way, showed great care and great skill. She is more than qualified to offer these beautiful lessons on service to all who want to help those hurting in this world.

As a person who works in a hospital, serves in ministry, has suffered loss, and has supported others through their losses, I know this book is needed. Michelle cares so authentically and deeply for people she sympathetically acts with purpose and helps others to do so. *Here for You* is a necessary education on how to serve others in their most vulnerable moments, with gentleness and thoughtfulness. Reflect on what is presented as you prepare yourself to do one of the greatest deeds you can do as a human being. To have compassion and give expression to it.

Nina L. Wooten

Acknowledgments

To God, who placed writing this book in my spirit, thank you for qualifying me and for helping me write this book from beginning to the end. Without You this book wouldn't have been possible.

To Paul, Thank you for allowing me the time to write this important book. It would have been tough without your prayers, patience, and understanding. To my sons, your impromptu hugs, kisses, and love while writing this book was everything I needed to keep going. You played a major part in my grieving journey, especially you Gabriel, you were so young. You knew the right time to give me hugs and kisses or to call me over to play with you. When I was in my head replaying my sorrows, you were the distraction I needed. You were who God used to help me move forward, the Lord manifested in flesh. I'll forever be grateful to God for you all.

To my Mom, thank you for introducing me to The Lord at an early age, showing me strength in the midst and how to pray and pick myself up after an unexpected blow in life. Your strength is unparalleled.

To Evanson and Vanity, we share the same grief and I thank you for the reminder to keep on living.

To Magda, thank you for being there during my initial grief. You have always been my cheerleader and encourager.

To my best friend Demitria, thank you for never missing a year to text me before the anniversary of Gloriana's death to see how I'm doing. Also, for encouraging me to write.

To my mother-in-law Jovonna Williams, thank you for being there when the initial grief hit our home. Your presence near and far was felt.

To my Pastors Derrick and Zelphia Raines, thank you for checking on me during my initial grief stage and the times after to make sure my mental state was still whole and intact. You didn't call to preach. You listened, then encouraged.

To Elder Anthony Moore who blessed us with the eulogy at Gloriana's memorial. I couldn't have picked a better person to speak that day.

To Deacon Nina Wooten, we share the same grief. Thank you for always reminding me in spite of what I've been through I still have light in me that shines.

To Zahria Raines, thank you for keeping me accountable in our talks about being who we're called to be.

To Traci Henderson-Smith, thank you for drawing out of me the desire I've always had to write.

To all who were in attendance for Gloriana's memorial, and all those who called thereafter checking on me. Thank you for your kindness, gentleness, and endearments.

ACKNOWLEDGMENTS

And last but not least my Editor, Covenant sister, my Minister, my Best Friend, words can't quantify or express my thank you. I'm grateful for all you've done and continue to do, especially during my grieving process. Love you. So glad it was you God chose to help me with this book.

Introduction

Death can hit like a category 5 hurricane, lifting, throwing, and ripping anything that isn't firmly anchored. Who we have around after the storm makes such a difference on how we process the aftermath. I know first-hand the importance of having a strong support system and how it can keep us standing firm long after tragedy ravages through our lives. This book is for the reader who knows anyone who was caught off guard by a death, unprepared for it, and who may be struggling to engage in life again.

Hindsight doesn't have to reveal the mysteries of grief. In this book you will receive the foresight of grief and how to be present as your loved ones heal during their bereavement. This book is also meant to be a guide to help you understand the journey of grief and to provide you with the most impactful and practical ways to be present.

Part I
GRIEF

Chapter 1

The Reality of Grief

No one anticipates grief. It's one of those things that linger, waiting to strike and slaps us out of nowhere. Death is a painful reminder that we were never meant to live on this earth forever. The reality is we'll all experience death and grief in our lifetime. Grief is not a one size fits all and no one is above experiencing it.

When death arrives, the grief that follows has the potential to change us and shift life as we know it. Some changes are subtle and we can miss it. However, some are in our face and we can't miss it even if we tried.

I've observed two ways grief can subtly change or shift us. One way is through our mental state which can look different for everyone. Some increase expressions of love in one moment and become forgetful and absent minded in the next. Before loss, we rightfully lived life as if grief wouldn't make its way to our doorstep. The goodbyes and hellos seemed to last forever, but when death happens it becomes a cruel reminder that death is real and is an ongoing possibility. It prompts us to make sure those around us know that they are loved. We begin to think and say things like, "Hey, you are very important to me" or "I can't imagine life without you" and "If I don't get to see you again, I want you to know that I love you."

When I was nine months pregnant with my second child, she passed away stillborn. I remember becoming numb to life and every passing day I would unknowingly go into a trance. When the initial grief subsided, I found myself constantly telling my first-born son I loved him and I wanted to be around him every moment.

Another change in my mental state was being distracted and forgetful. Repetitive, everyday tasks seemed to be a non-issue but tasks that needed my full attention, concentration, or much of my effort were forgotten or done haphazardly. I would forget important dates and birthdays all while putting on a smile for everyone around me. I pushed on to live a normal life outwardly but there were subtle signs that grief had changed me like so many others. For some it can be wanting to sleep all day or managing feelings of exhaustion. I remember crying once because the weather had changed. Everything can feel like a big deal even when it's small, and unexpected disruptions could trigger an emotional response. All of these can reveal subtle shifts in our mental state.

The second way I've observed grief subtly changing or shifting in a person is through their outlook on life. Some feel they were robbed or betrayed by their loss. Not only robbed of the person they loved but robbed of the life they'd imagined they'd have. Others can begin to be angry with themselves, with others, with institutions, and even with God. Life for them can begin to feel cold and dark. What was once considered to be a beautiful life now seems an empty shell of what life has become.

These are the realities of grief and it's not only reserved for the moment. It can come and go over the course of a lifetime. Since the grieving process is different for everyone, the pain of losing a loved one can be constant or a slow release. Some replay memories of their loved one constantly in their mind because of their deep felt love for them but this can also bring constant pain. Some memories come back in increments; returning in bits and pieces when visiting shared places, familiar encounters, and remembering hopes they once had with those they loved.

Growing up I personally didn't give much thought to death. It wasn't until one of my favorite uncles died that I had my first experience with grief. I remember laying down in my bedroom and hearing my mother speaking inaudibly down the hallway. After what felt like 30 minutes, she walked in and told me my uncle passed away. His death was sudden. I don't remember the questions I asked but I do remember turning towards the wall and the tears welling up instantly.

Years later when my daughter died, I experienced intimate grief. Her stillbirth was bitter for me. The grief was so heavy I couldn't get my heart and my brain to get in sync. As if my heart and brain were having a conversation about me while I was in the room. My heart would say, "Michelle this shook your whole world but God is still on the throne of your life and He will get you through this." However, my brain would say, "If there was a God then why would He put you through this? Why would he let such a tragedy happen on His watch?" My Heart would rebuttal with "She didn't really die. She lives in heaven now." I felt like a bystander watching my heart and soul try to grasp and understand what's happening while I tried to decide which I agreed with.

When I think of how far I've come, I don't know how I could've made it through without God and the people in my corner supporting me. I remember the grieving process taking longer than I expected as I kept falling apart over and over again. However, there did come a time when I didn't fall apart. It felt like an awakening. All of a sudden the feeling of gray skies hovering over me was gone. I felt refreshed. I had a brand new outlook and desire to socialize again with family and friends. I would accept invitations to parties and go to events. My hope returned to me and I began to feel okay again. I would still cry from time to time but it didn't stop me from re-emerging to engage in life again, especially with my family. I was so grateful for those who partnered with me and supported me while I grieved.

Chapter 2

The Idea of Moving On

There is often an expectation that once someone has grieved that they will be the same person afterwards, but that's not the case. Grief has a way of causing us to sometimes act out on impulses. We may do or say things we don't mean. Some don't want to listen to reasoning. Others lash out at anyone who tries to help them. Many things can contribute to this behavior; lack of sleep, anger, or even a sense of the world owing them something for their pain. Grief can cause a person to be less sensitive or very sensitive or some variation of both. Either way, we should not rush the grieving process by insisting they move on.

Sometimes rushing a person in the grieving process is perceived as wanting the person to erase the memory of their loved one. The grief process can be delicate and saying whatever comes to mind about moving on can be perturbing and could knock the griever off the little ground they have left underneath them. When my daughter passed, I remember talking to a family member on the phone the day I got back from the hospital. I remember crying and telling them how this was so unfair. The person said "You know crying over this baby that died won't bring her back. You're young and healthy. You can get pregnant again if you wanted to." Their response was not what I needed to hear at the time. I thought I had an ear to vent to release some of the pain but that wasn't the case, they wanted me to get over it. Hearing those words felt like I was pushed off the highest skyscraper. I cut the call short and decided to stay off the phone for days. That day I realized the importance of being allowed to have my moment. Like so many others, I wasn't ready to move on. People need a safe place to voice their pain. Otherwise it can feel debilitating when there is pressure on every side to be 'normal' again.

I believe when a griever rushes their grieving process, it takes them back to unfinished business the past has with them. It's like going to a room to retrieve something but forgetting only to remember minutes later and having to go back to retrieve it all over again. Taking the time to properly grieve is like sitting in the room unhurriedly and thinking about what it was that brought you to the room in the first place. A griever is entitled to move on at their pace, they define what pace they would like to take. Our goal should be to encourage them along the way.

It's easy to think grief heals like a physical wound. It's tempting to assume because the scar has a scab that the process has ended. I remember reading an article on advancedtissue.com, The Signs and Stages of Wound Healing, after my c-section, and they mentioned healing could possibly last for years even after the wound has scabbed over. The scab is just there to close the wound so it doesn't get infected on the inside. I believe the grief process is similar. Grief is a scab that others can see but we should recognize that there is still healing that needs to be done beneath the surface.

Moving on from the grieving process can be a sore subject. I've heard people on the outside looking in say things like, "They should have moved on a long time ago" or "It's been 10 years, they should have already moved on." I believe what they were really trying to convey was something a friend said to me once. "There is a difference between grieving and laying in grief." When she shared this with me, it opened my eyes to what grieving is truly about. Grieving gives us the opportunity to sort things out in life and become centered. However, lying in grief is more like giving up on hope. The desire is not to be consoled or come to a place of wholeness but to lay in the hurt and do nothing about it. A person in that hopeless state doesn't want to meet with anyone or even begin to get centered again. It seems like a resolve to make grief life. Although it's tempting for many grievers to do this, it's never beneficial. And while I agree everyone deserves to reach a healthy place post-grief where they don't feel like falling apart every moment; that moment arrives at different times for different people. My hope for those who grieve is for them to maintain their hope for wholeness again. Those supporting someone in the grief process can gently remind them that there is hope available to them for healing and deliverance in their own time.

Part II
THE ART OF BEING PRESENT

Chapter 3

Identifying Your Motivation

Our motives should be pure and clear on why we want to help. Do we truly want to help? If so, in what ways? Is it to add to their lives to combat the grief, to become a part of their healing process, or to be a positive encounter for them? Time is a precious commodity and deciding to help others can be a sacrifice. There's nothing like someone giving of themselves and wanting nothing in return especially for those who have nothing they could give in return. When you are motivated to help someone simply because your heart breaks for them, you begin to embody what love truly is.

If you're motivated to add to someone, there are many ways you can accomplish that. It can be easy to offer empty condolences and verbally say, "I am here if you need me." Although this is a good gesture, it can be misinterpreted without corresponding action. Actions can speak louder than words so when your motivation comes from a sincere place, then being there for the person translates very well. Adding to someone can be as simple as going the extra mile for them. Whether it be calling them routinely to check on them or sending meals so they have one less thing to do; these actions communicate you are here for them and you want to lift burdens.

Chapter 4

Being Present

Being present to listen without judging speaks louder than frustrated or unsure words. A strong quiet presence can help the griever tremendously and it won't run the risk of being shut out. After my daughter passed, my best friend took leave from her job on the day I was released from the hospital and was on a plane the same day just to sit by my side. During her entire visit, she never initiated a discussion about the death of my daughter. She and my sister just silently sat with me. I appreciated that so much. They spoke when I asked them questions about what was going on in their lives. Almost as if we were on the same wavelength. They knew when to talk and when to sit quietly and be present and they never made it awkward. One particular memory still brings a smile to my face. I remember my best friend, my sister, and I sitting at my dining room table. My best friend proceeded to tell me about all the hilarious stories and videos going viral on social media. She subtly brought the social aspect of the world back into my world after I shut the world out. It was skillful, subtle, and brief. We also played many rounds of my favorite card game. We laughed and whenever I had a moment and would cry, the whole room allowed me space to grieve and I was able to cry unapologetically. I felt safe. That feeling, their presence, and the distraction of good company was needed. It felt good to escape my thoughts and to know I was surrounded by love.

Making ourselves available and learning how to be present is an extension of love. While healing is taking place, the griever needs physical arms to hug them, gentle eyes giving them loving attention, compassionate voices to comfort them, and willing supporters present to remind them they are not alone. Present helpers are a necessity.

Chapter 5

Exercising Patience

Some of the best helpers are those who learn how to exercise unwavering patience. When our interactions become predictable it can result in the person we're supporting feeling safe and at ease. Patience being consistently extended towards me enabled me to view death differently. There's a beautiful process called metamorphosis that takes place when we have friends and family covering us in loving patience during our cocoon of grief. It's like curtains covering our vulnerability. It takes time to undress all the pain, sadness, guilt, misconception and confusion that comes with death. Having patient people around who don't judge our grief is important. Judgement can lead to stagnation. The griever can get so busy defending or protecting themselves they don't truly get time to heal and their progress can become stunted.

My husband and friends were patient with me when my daughter passed away. They gave way to me in times of frustration. Allowing me to be whatever I needed to be during the grief, even pardoning me when I got out of line. One day during a grief episode, I found myself talking extremely bad about a person and just putting them in a bad light but later when I apologized for my negativity they assured me what I said wouldn't make them look at the person any differently, calming my anxiety of hurting that person's image. I found most grievers may not be able to process or filter their words before they say them, but later come to their senses and try to make things right. I'm not advocating poor behavior or being somewhere you're being abused. I'm saying to keep their grief in mind and move gently and fluidly. Operate in love while making your boundaries known but extend patience until they return to soundness.

Being patient means learning how to minimize your frustration when you're trying to help. If you find yourself frustrated when the griever doesn't show signs of what we consider progress or they're taking longer to come out of the initial stage of grief, don't think this is a reflection of you or let it cause insecurities in you. Take a step back and evaluate what's going on internally. Remember, this is their journey and you're the light to help them see their way. My husband once said to me during a conversation about the hurting people in the world, "Patience is something often needed but seldom found. There are so many people with lingering unseen relational wounds simply because patience was in short supply."

Chapter 6

Extending Empathy

When we extend empathy to someone in grief we don't just commiserate with them we aim to understand firsthand what it must be like to walk in their shoes. It helps us to identify the best way we can step into the trenches with them and get involved in their new world without their loved one. An important part of extending empathy is allowing the person grieving to vocalize their perspective on what they are feeling. I've heard some say it feels like a punishment being left behind to hurt and suffer. Others may say it's a day of glory. Their loved one finally gained their wings and is no longer suffering. It's important to acknowledge both feelings as valid. It is their perspective to have and we need to be considerate of how they view and process the grief. You don't have to agree to be supportive. Empathy is a skill that makes us more intuitive and others-minded. A griever remembers an empathetic person. They remember how easy it was to be around them and how comfortable they were opening up to an empathetic person because it made them feel safe. However, empathy should be exercised with boundaries. I realized when I'm around grief, I can get caught up in my own emotions. I would relate too deeply to their grief and in my emotionalism I became more of a distraction than a support. This can cause the spotlight to be taken off of the griever and placed on us, pushing the griever to the side, and making us the center of attention. There should always be a balance when we are sharing the griever's emotion. We should empathize enough help to the griever but not to the extent that we're falling apart and needing encouragement too.

Chapter 7

Practical Ways to Help

There are many different ways we can help those grieving and we can get creative in the type of support we give. I remember my mother-in-law flying in town after the passing of our daughter. When she arrived, she helped my husband set up our daughter's cremation and helped prepare the memorial service. As I thought about it months later, I was grateful for her and what she did. When we thoughtfully help a griever, that kind of support is hard to forget.

One way we can help is through gifts and engagement. While some may need a month or two to regain their desire to engage in activities, others may want to occupy their mind until they get their footing. The goal is not to keep them occupied 24/7 so they don't grieve but to help guide them into the grieving journey. Keep in mind they may have triggers that could remind them of their loved one during the activity so be mindful and wise when choosing something thoughtful. Here is a short list of engaging or therapeutic gifts, activities, and services that may be beneficial to explore.

Therapeutic Gifts & Activities
- Buy them a journal. This can be used to express their feelings.
- Purchase a pet they've always talked about.
- Order a plant growing kit or sign them up for a plant growing or gardening class.
- Pay for a session with a very good therapist or counselor.
- Gift them a spa treatment.
- Give them gift cards.
- Give them money.

Services
- Gift them a housekeeping service for a month.
- Have essentials, favorite food and groceries delivered to their home.
- Offer to help them run important errands.
- Help or link them with someone who can help them start a blog, nonprofit, charity or organization.

PRACTICAL WAYS TO HELP

Engaging Activities

- Purchase a train, bus or a plane ticket to another city or island.
- Go with them to the movies to watch a comedy.
- Take them to a stand-up comedy show.
- Reserve seats to a painting class together or buy art canvas kit and bring painting class to them.
- Take them hiking, camping or on an adventure.

Part III
CONSIDERATIONS

Chapter 8

Identifying When we Can't Help

There may come a time when we are not in a good place to help others. Maybe we don't have the patience or the emotional energy to be what is needed in that moment. We might be too rash with our responses, too distant while in their presence, or too tired to follow through when we say we will do something. In close proximity it's easy to do damage with our words or actions when we're just trying to help. However, we also need to understand it's okay to accept that we can't always help in the way we'd like to. It's better to acknowledge that before we align ourselves with someone's grieving journey. Fortunately, there are other ways to help. Maybe we can refer them to a qualified therapist or group support to ensure they get the help they need.

If you consider yourself to be a spiritual person or a believer in God, another way to help is through prayer. I truly believe prayer can shift the spiritual landscape of a person's life. Releasing what we can't do in the natural to God who is supernatural is powerful in heaven and earth. Set a reminder on your calendar to lift them up in prayer. This is done behind the scenes for the person grieving. Be okay praying in private and this going unnoticed by the griever. The goal is not to be acknowledged by them for your prayers. It's knowing power beyond the natural is needed to help in areas we can't.

An indirect way we can help is by offering monetary support. We can convey love and a desire to help when we can't in our usual ways by helping with funeral expenses, meals, groceries, or bills. Our money can stand in as a representative, communicating that we don't want them burdened with too many cares as they grieve.

We should carefully consider what we can do to support, once we've identified we can't offer traditional help. We don't want to completely disconnect from supporting our loved one in grief. We can continue to be thoughtful, resourceful, prayerful, or financially supportive. We do what we have the capacity to do, whether it is through direct or indirect support.

Chapter 9

When They Don't Want to Talk

When someone is grieving, talking can be the last thing they want to do. In those cases, we can approach as a gardener. We can plant seeds of love and water them with our presence and when they are ready, they will step into the sunlight again. What we don't want to do is pressure them to talk.

If we don't know how to help or tried but were pushed away or aggressively reprimanded then we should step back and reevaluate. Maybe they have entered a new stage of grief or they're experiencing so much emotional and mental pain they don't want to engage right now. This maybe the time for you to give them the space and the time to process and purge in solitude. We can engage again when they are in a better space to receive us. Also, keep in mind we may not be the form of help that person needs at the moment. We shouldn't take it personal. They may be doing their best to find a way to cope or to find stability. Let's not turn our hearts away but continue our unconditional support and care for them.

Also, just because a person doesn't want to talk doesn't mean they're opposed to hearing us talk. Sometimes hearing how their loved ones positively impacted us or others can bring some joy and even laughter. Every person touched by the death of a loved one carries the memory of them and how they saw them. Hearing someone speak about them in the way they remember them can be refreshing. Let's be patient for when they are ready to talk again. They will be sure to let us know.

Chapter 10

Avoiding Trigger Words

It's human nature to try to help when someone is hurting. However, we can often end up saying the wrong thing or saying something at the wrong time. We want to avoid wounding the grieving with our words creating something else they need to heal from. Every action and word matters and can't be taken back once it's been said. There were a few people who felt the need to use words that weren't carefully thought out during my initial grief period and it caused me great anger. To be fair, I'm sure I've misspoken before saying trigger words to a griever. We are humans and we'll make mistakes. I've found using fewer words to be the best approach. More talking leads to more chances to say the wrong things. Saying the wrong thing has a way of haunting us with regret but even worst, haunting the griever with pain.

When we don't know what to say it can be easy to rely on social cues. Social cues have taught us to say things like, "Sorry for your loss" but then we go on with life disconnecting from the person grieving. We never take the opportunity to learn better ways to navigate grief and especially how to support those who grieve. Rather than relying on social cues, we can glean wisdom from 1 Peter 3:8-12 (MSG), "Be agreeable, be sympathetic, be loving, be compassionate, be humble. That goes for all of us, no exceptions. No retaliation. No sharp-tongued sarcasm." I've found this to be words to live by.

Chapter 11

Speaking Life into Grief

An invitation to speak into the griever's life is an invitation of trust and speaking life into grief will require learning to become a skillful listener. A keen listener isn't quick to speak, quick to offer advice, or quick to correct for every vent. We should carefully evaluate our motives and words paying attention to moods, emotions, and changes in behavior before, during, and after we share. If we listen well, we know the griever will lead us in what they need. How we handle the initial invitation will determine whether or not we get another chance to speak into their lives.

When we support the grieving, we should consider ourselves a temple where they want to come to get healed. We want them to feel alive when they're with us and feel a sense of lifting and peace once they depart. Our presence as a peaceful, safe place can impart life into grief sometimes that even the most gentle words cannot. Audible words or not, we can be confident we are injecting life into their grief.

Conclusion

We will always have the hurting among us, however the weight of this thought shouldn't overwhelm us. Our goal isn't to heal, it's to be patiently present with our love in the midst of the broken pieces until the puzzle of life reconnects. It's not always the power of words but our gentle expressions and actions that are needed. We can allow others to grieve at their own pace, walking alongside them as they brace for the journey towards healing. It's not an inconvenience but a privilege to support in any way.

Life offers us all highs and lows. May we each have the courage to respond to their lows with a sincere and gentle, "I'm here for you. What can I do to help?"

Reference

"The Signs and Stages of Wound Healing", September 9, 2014, advancedtissue.com, Copyright © 2014 Advanced Tissue, https://advancedtissue.com/2014/09/signswound-healing-stages/, (p.11)

Holy Bible, The Message Translation. NavPress Publishing Group, Copyright © 1993, 1994, 1995, 1996, 2001, 2002 (1 Peter 3:8-12), (p. 38)

In Loving Memory

Gloriana Evonna Harris, Barbara Morin, Zoë Paige Morin, Baby Boy Wooten, Granmè Mamalo, Uncle Enoch Morin, Predilia (Tou-Toune) JeanPierre, and all those who left us before we were ready to let go and those who will leave before our hearts are ready to say goodbye.

www.ingramcontent.com/pod-product-compliance
Lightning Source LLC
Chambersburg PA
CBHW020915080526
44589CB00011B/601